These words are dedicated to:

My fruits Amaris and Sabu II
and the tree that stands strong beside
me, Sabu

maktüb

"I've counted the moons until you were mine, yet before, time never existed…"

"Baba"

I put my ear to a glass in hopes I would hear
you clearly

Yelled "Are you there?" in a room with just me

Asked the trees if they heard any sign from you

They simply just waved in the breeze

A lady bug flew and landed on the top of my nose

Maybe that's the only confirmation I'll need

Just when I thought your voice wouldn't be heard
after all

The rain cried "Now you have listened to me".

*"Arriving to the moment
where you've imagined things
twice,*

is understanding who truly
holds the power... "

"Rhythm"

If an hourglass measures time, so can it account
for my many tears

The many steps I've walked to reach you

The excitement and also my fears

If time can be measured, shall it tally up my glee

The gratitude I feel every morning simply just to
be

But what is time really, but a measure of our
day

The weeks, months, even years to come

 Just the sun and moon racing to play

"I've used these same tears to water the seeds I've prayed over.

The harvest tastes even more sweet. . ."

"Changes"

I've watched winter melt,

Spring bloom,

Summer shine,

While Autumn makes room.

I've grown with each season,

Transforming my life.

As night becomes day and day
becomes night.

"There's a bird who sings every morning,

her song the sound of the journey she's flown. . ."

"Afflatus"

Tell me,

Does the moon and sun bow at your presence

While stars align asking for your grace

Knowing that you possess so much power

Attention fixed when you walk into the place

You wear a crown never tilting

A garment demanding much respect

Allow me to be your muse

Your greatest creation yet.

"Sand is part of the ocean,

But never the ocean part of

sand. . ."

"*Rebirth*"

I am no better than the flower that
dies in the fall,

That withers from the cold, then
seems forever lost.

I am *just* like that flower, grown from
a seed,

blooming each springtime, my
mother the bearing tree.

"Sunflower"

My sweet, sweet boy

We've made you with so much love.

You're a creation from smiles,
kisses, laughs, and all our hugs.

I named you long before when you
were just a prayer of mine

When I questioned if I was worthy, if
I deserved a gift so divine.

You chose us I'm sure of this, how
else could this be.

Our perfect little sunflower, grown
all from just a seed.

"As a parent I thought I would be the teacher,

you come to realize, your child is the true leader…"

"What is the difference between a child's bravery and elasticity for hope,

than an adult who 's been left to try life unafraid and alone…"

"*Initiation*"

This new body gets hot quickly,

or is it just me?

Not to mention all the nectar that spills
over dripping down past my belly.

I can't catch up on rest, no matter how
hard I've tried

I promise I'm stronger than this, but
every day I seem to cry.

There are some days when I feel
overwhelmed, I'm not proud to admit

They say it takes a village, but that's
something I ain't get

Yet, when I look at my baby all my
worries cover and hide

. . .

(…*"Initiation"* continued)

I stand up

Wipe my face

Put aside my pride

This body was made to do just exactly

what it did.

My mind is strong and capable,

My heart has grown so big.

Though the introduction to motherhood
can sometimes seem so tough

My babies are worth it, living proof of all
our love

"Be gentle with yourself,

You deserve just as much

grace. . ."

"Nanna Say"

Am I strong because you've labelled me
as such?

I have weak moments even though I say
that I'm tough.

What?

Did you expect me to cry, while my hands
were already full?

Ask for tissue while I drown in this tear-
made pool?

I guess I'm strong ain't I?

Nobody asks if I'm okay.

"Chile, ain't no sense in fussin' bout it no

way", that's what Nanna say!

"Hair Salon"

Does it have to hurt?

These coils and kinks

My neck, your back

Bathtubs, kitchen

sinks

Does it have to hurt

so bad? Can you just

put it in a bun? I don't

mind if it starts to loc

Maybe that will be fun

My scalp is so tender

I'm only just five

I do love the braids

(…*"Hair Salon"* continued)

Twist

Oh, and the one ponytail to the side

But Mom why does it hurt so bad; I
can't stop screaming "owww."

I can't take it anymore

"Mommmm"

"Stoppp"

…

But wait "oOoo look at my crown".

"It was my daughter's happiness that healed the broken child I've been nurturing. . ."

"Nostalgia"

Remember Double Dutch, handball,
dice, hopscotch, hula-hoops!

Quarter waters, Debbie cakes,
crybabies, and cheese doodles

Bamboo earrings, 5 percenters,
beepers, hoagies for lunch

Project hallways, boombox blasting,
playing numbers of out luck

When Nas had plans to rule the
world and took Lauryn from
DownTheHill

There's nothing like back in the day,
the 90's had all the feels

"Brown Girl"

Brown girl,

You are made of gold and cinnamon

amber, molasses, and myrrh.

Bark of the strong Baobab tree,

cocoa with a sprinkle of dirt

You glow under God's light

Shimmer like sand at the beach

So many shades of beautiful brown

Just look in the mirror and see

"Reflection"

Will it shatter knowing her truth

After all, it's seen her reflection

at its worse

She can't stand the sight of

her tears

So she avoids eye contact at all

cost

It knows her strengths,
weaknesses, flaws,

and unmentioned cons

How the mirror can be so unkind

"Do not be afraid to try,

Be afraid of never finding the

courage. . ."

"*Me vs Me*"

I've felt uneasy with myself before
knowing this discomfort

Having many disagreements with the
reflection I banter with

Who's right between my voice and
the echoes heard

Battling uncertainty

"Facing It"

I've tried on many faces all fitting
with room for growth

None just quite perfect, but still
trying on with much hope

Some that fit can use adornment to
speak of my eclectic rhyme

I've worn these many faces for you,
yet none of them truly mine

"Loudest Whispers"

I know I'm the best

I've worked so hard for this

More people should know who I am

It's the quiet confidence screaming to
be heard, but I hush her and keep
her in

I'm worth more than they know

Who can compete with me?

This credence I carry will no longer
                              keep quiet

It's the words I whisper, yet they

sound so loud, but they seem safer
inside

"The rain seemed like the end, until a rainbow began to show…"

"You will only receive the truth, when you are open to accepting your lies…"

"Emotions"

When anger speaks in tongues it
chokes while gasping for grace

Sadness cries as it begs for
happiness

Disappointment is only yearning for
acceptance

Regret demanding for revision
called change

*"As the drop of water trickles down
to finally meet the sea,*

*we must not rush our fate the
inevitable
called*

destiny... "

"I do today, I did yesterday, and I always will. . ."

"In-Yun"

Are we not connected by invisible strings
of fate and moments of coincidence?

Like the bird that broke the tree and used
its branch to build its home

The rain that nourished the plants and
quenched the thirst of many animals.

The mountain that was once just a sheet of
snow

Many timelines and different journeys
leading to the same space.

The brush of our shoulders was the
moment of know,

Yet, you've changed my course of
trajectory.

This moment simply painted *In-Yun.*

"Distance is no true suitor for a connection tied with the fibers of our soul. . ."

"Senses"

"His voice touches me in ways, better than his fingers have.

The kiss he gave sang to my heart.

The taste of his scent never leaving my lips

His eyes read *"May we never part"*

"*Celestial*"

Her hips whisper sweet melodies

Forgiving me for the pain emulated
as pleasure

I push between her thighs

Giving only what she asked for

Her screams demanding, inviting my
body and mind

She's unworldly drifting between
galaxies and I'm the rocket taking
her

High, high, high

"Sex isn't just an action, but an abyss that I sink to with my legs spread wide willing to receive and release my nature's honeydew.

And boy I've been dripping!!"

"Farewell Kiss"

May your words be the last I hear

Your smile the last I see

A hug is the sweetest touch from you

The final kiss farewell to me

Though I know I've borrow you for long

You were never mine to keep

How God has been so generous

To give your heart to me.

"Greatest Gift"

Is it the warmth I feel as I gaze in your eyes

Or the curve you've placed on my face called a smile

The comfort I feel lets me know that I'm safe

I find heaven in your heart others imagine the place

Gentle like doves, but rich as gold's value

Years before lost, thank God I have found you

You're perfect to me every inch of your being

You are by far the greatest gift that I have been given

*"Art is the language of many
who speak without words,*

yet listen with their mind…"

"Virgo"

Perfectionist

But didn't mama tell you there's no such thing?

Overthinking questioning what you've observed

You won't call it judgmental,

But there is just this one thing

Giving credit to the detailed eye

You know the difference between a painting and true art

Success never seems to be far

After all, your ruler dances closest to the biggest star

(… *"Virgo"* continued)

If you could travel out of your

own head, Where's the first

place you would go?

I see you in the night sky

constellation

… the stars call you Virgo

"Daedalus' Mistake"

I touched it!

Flew high above the trees and
flighted birds

Way out into blue solace where
nothing can be heard

Out into the atmosphere way up
above

Past the planet that's slated grey
and the planet of love

I did, I touched it, please say you

believe me!

My wings never felt this

much grace

(…"*Daedalus" Mistake*"   continued)

With breath in my lungs

Light in my eyes

Breeze brushing against my face

The sun's light so bold and
luminous
This piece I've brought back say
you'll take
Icarus could never compare to me
I know of Daedalus' mistake

"We may read the same book,

but surely, we have viewed different editions . . ."

"Sand trickling one grain at a time

Wind swiftly brushing through trees

Water pouring and flowing to Great
Lakes and rivers

Patience is nature's true purpose to
be. . ."

"Moon's Canvas"

The night sky brings something
promising
Knowing sunshine will ultimately
exist
There's a secrecy we both share
A quiet truth needing no reveal
Sharing more than complexion
Holding more than emotions
Both celestial and full of shine

"The glass only became half
full, once I poured into
myself. . ."

"The Leap"

As if I balanced on a tight rope hung
from the heavens above

Then jumped with all my might, not
having anything to be afraid of

Packed all my self doubt and baggage
and shipped it on its way

I had something to prove to myself
now that I'm braver than yesterday

It's scary holding a seed and praying
that it grows with strength

But I've mustarded up the courage
and took the leap of faith

ACKNOWLEDGMENTS

Thank you to my amazing family
for being the muses behind this
piece of work.

To Sabu, I thank you for loving me with
enough romance to feel such deep
emotions of unconditional love,
happiness,
and support. For years of love
letters dedicated to you and many
more to come. And for the amazing
artwork you have created for these
pages and in my life every day.

Amaris, my princess you are the
inspiration for Brown Girl and so
many other works. You are the
best pinky-promise best friend I could
ask for. Sabu II, my golden sunflower,
thank you for being a bright twinkle in
my eyes. I love you both more than the
moon, sun, and stars in the sky.

Nanna, my matriarch I thank you
for the daily phone calls that
allow me to gain so much wisdom,
knowledge, and plenty of laughs. I
love you deep and always
thinking of you beautiful.

Mama, thank you for always wanting to
see me win. You are proof of resilience,
God's love, and answered prayers. Thank
you for all the love you have filled me
with so I can pour it back into the world.

Daci, thank you for being God's
confirmation when I needed to be uplifted
and hear God even more clearly. Thank
you for pushing me to take this leap of
faith and holding my hand as we float!

Reader, I am full of gratitude and thankful
beyond words for your support. May you
have continued peace, love, and
abundance.

Never Sleep on God!

* 9 7 9 8 2 1 8 4 7 0 3 3 3 *